IMAGES
of America

ROAD TO RAINIER SCENIC BYWAY

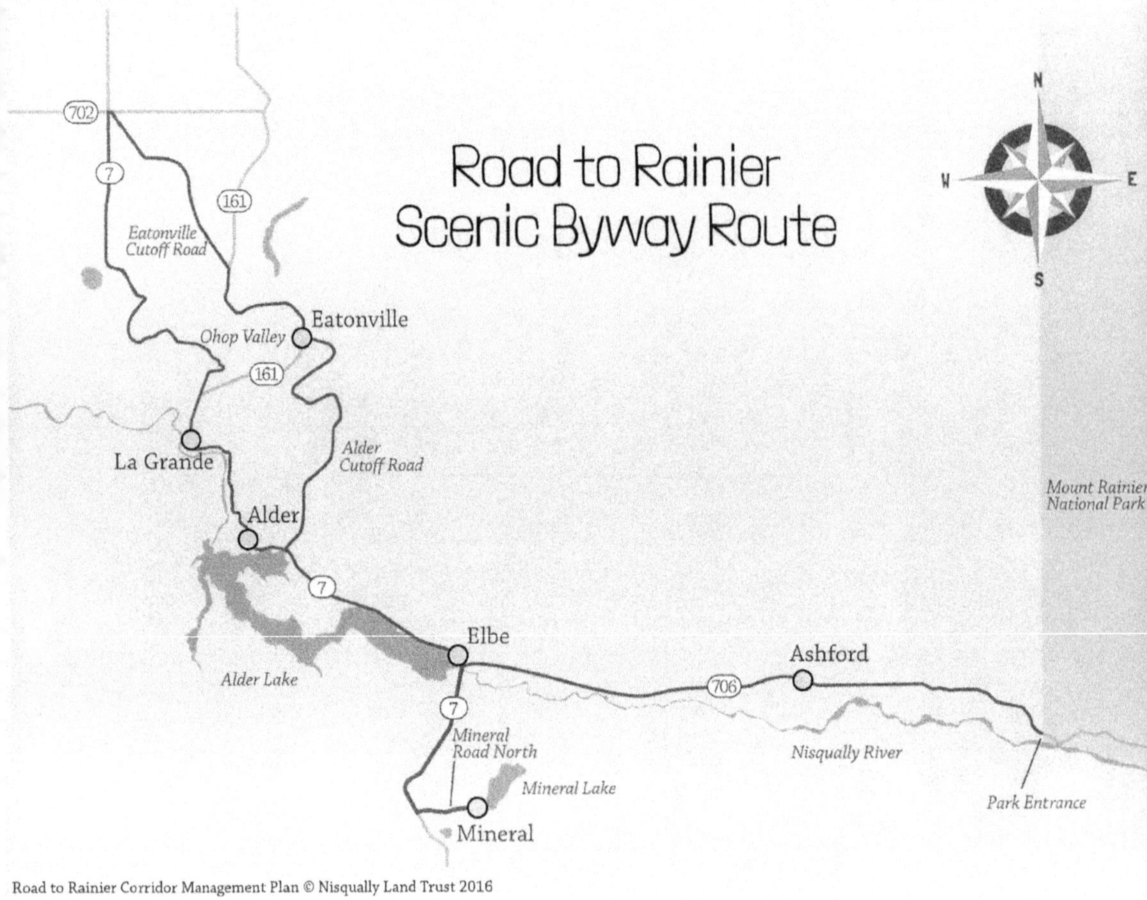

Pictured here is the Road to Rainier Scenic Byway map, as included in the Corridor Management Plan prepared by Sarah Scott. (Nisqually Land Trust.)

On the Cover: This 12-seat Buick convertible serves as a stage, transporting guests from Mineral, Elbe, and Ashford to Paradise Valley. (Tacoma Public Library G76.1.067.)

IMAGES
of America

ROAD TO RAINIER SCENIC BYWAY

Donald M. Johnstone and the
South Pierce County Historical Society

ARCADIA
PUBLISHING

ISBN 978-1-4671-2928-2

Published by Arcadia Publishing
Charleston, South Carolina

Library of Congress Control Number: 2018932466

For all general information, please contact Arcadia Publishing:
Telephone 843-853-2070
Fax 843-853-0044
E-mail sales@arcadiapublishing.com
For customer service and orders:
Toll-Free 1-888-313-2665

Visit us on the Internet at www.arcadiapublishing.com

Contents

ACKNOWLEDGMENTS

There are many groups, individuals, and families behind this project who deserve my thanks. Pat Van Eaton has spent several years scanning the photograph albums of many pioneer families, creating the South Pierce County Historical Society's digital collection. Bob Walter and Roni Johnson and other members of the society were particularly helpful to verify facts, read captions, and select photographs. The forestry consultants were Bob Johnstone and Dick and Paula Hopkins. I thank Rich and Ruthie Williams, who shared their photograph collection and love of Eatonville history.

A number of people, agencies, and institution have helped me find informative or historical photographs: Jin Yi of Tacoma Public Utilities; Nancy Barker, Elbe unit public use manager of the Washington State Department of Natural Resources; Eileen Price of the Washington State Historical Society; the staff of the Northwest Room of the Tacoma Public Library; Rebecca Baker, University of Washington Libraries/Special Collections; and the staff of the Eatonville Branch of the Pierce County Library System.

Individuals and families have been extremely generous in sharing their photographs, as well as their memories and stories. The Eatonville and Ohop families who have contributed to the historical society's digital collection include, but are not limited to, the Bloom, Boettcher, Borden, Christensen, Haynes, Hendersen, King, Kjelstad, Langberg, Lewis, Mettler, Peterson, Sakura, Taylor, and Van Eaton families. Many of the Flynn and Mineral photographs are from Jim and Edie Hale, who have been collecting old photographs for many years. Jim, in his 90s, would dive under the bed to retrieve another box of treasures every time he thought of another story.

Special thanks go to my title manager, Caroline Anderson of Arcadia Publishing, who cheerfully guided me through the whole publishing process. Heidi Waterhouse did a great job organizing the text and correcting the grammar.

Most especially, I would like to thank my wife, Kathy, and the family who looked at the pictures as they came in and made time for me to do all the work that needed to be done. Thank you.

Unless otherwise noted, all images appear courtesy of the South Pierce County Historical Society.

The following institutions have granted permission for the use of their images in this publication. To minimize the length of citations, the following abbreviations are used:

MOHAI: Museum of History & Industry Photograph Collection
TPU: Tacoma Public Utilities
TPL: Tacoma Public Library
UofW: University of Washington Libraries, Special Collections
WSDOT: Washington State Department of Transportation
WSHS: Washington State Historical Society

Introduction

A scenic byway is a unique type of transportation corridor. The purpose is not speed, congestion relief, or getting from point-to-point. A scenic byway exists to remind the traveler to slow down, look around, learn something new, and enjoy the drive. To earn the designation of "scenic byway," a Washington State highway corridor is nominated by some group with local community ties. The byway must comply with program limitations and meet the specified criteria. There are different kinds of designated highways: historical, cultural, or memorial. They all have different standards but must all have at least some access to a part of a public park, forest, shoreline, recreational area, or national monument, and the majority of the route must be located in unincorporated areas.

The criteria by which a scenic route is evaluated include subjective standards relating to beauty, education, or historical value. The scenic standard is that it "have a heightened visual experience offering a pleasing and memorable visual experience." Anyone who has turned a corner and seen Mount Rainier—or as the locals call it, "the Mountain"—may agree that it is memorable. Those who have seen the Mountain come out from behind the clouds to reflect the winter sunlight off new-fallen snow may remember it for years. Those watching on a summer evening as the colors of the Mountain go from glacial white, to sunset yellow, to alpenglow pink and purple, and finally, to a ghostly shadow blocking the stars will remember the ethereal beauty of the mountain with cities at its skirts.

The Road to Rainier Scenic Byway was the product of a committee of local groups and individuals working together to improve the experience of visitors to and from the Nisqually Entrance of Mount Rainier National Park. The membership has changed over time but has included members from the Pierce County government, Mount Rainier Railroad & Logging Museum, Eatonville Chamber of Commerce, Nisqually Indian Tribe, Visit Rainier, Whittaker Mountaineering, Nisqually River Foundation, Washington State Department of Transportation, Mount Rainier Visitor Association, Ohop Grange, and the Pioneer Farm. The Corridor Management Plan was prepared by Sarah Scott and used extensively in this work. I am very appreciative of the quality of her work.

The Road to Rainier began hundreds, if not thousands, of years ago, as Native Americans of the area developed a system of north–south trails that followed the foothills of the Cascade Range and connected settlements and resources. These met with other trails that crossed the Cascades and permitted a system of trade to develop between the communities on Puget Sound, those along the Columbia River, and beyond.

The first recorded European visitor to Mount Rainier was William Fraser Tolmie. He was born in Scotland and graduated from the University of Glasgow with a medical degree. He joined the Hudson's Bay Company and was assigned to Fort Vancouver in the Oregon Territory. Soon after arriving in 1833, he was sent north to establish a new trading post where the Nisqually River enters Puget Sound. After the stockade and post were complete, he took an excursion up the Puyallup and Carbon Rivers to the snowfields on the lower slopes of Mount Rainier where he touched a glacier and collected botany samples. A lifelong journalist, Tolmie recorded his journey overland from the Columbia River to Puget Sound, an earthquake, and the first European's picnic at Mount Rainier.

Until the end of the American Civil War, there was a slow trickle of European and American settlers entering the Puget Sound region. Most of the Europeans and Canadians were with the Hudson's Bay Company and were interested in the company's businesses—first exploring and beaver trapping and then later farming and ranching. The Americans came to see how they could make their fortunes out of the wilderness, but most were not fortunate. In 1853, James Longmire used a portion of the Native American trail system to lead a wagon train from Walla Walla to the south bank of the Nisqually River. Over the next 30 years, he explored around Mount Rainier and guided people and parties as they did scientific research and frolicked on the Mountain.

In 1884, James Longmire discovered a hot spring near the upper reaches of the Nisqually River, which became known as Longmire Springs. He built a small house/hotel and let it be known that he was accepting paying guests. There were two main routes to the springs. One followed a trail established by a local Indian guide, Indian Henry, in the 1860s. It left from both Tacoma and Steilacoom, went south past Spanaway Lake, wound around hills and lakes until it reached what now is Elbe on the Nisqually River, and then headed up along the river to the hotel. The second route left Yelm on the lower Nisqually and traveled upriver to Ohop Creek and along the creek until it met the trail coming down from Tacoma. The La Grande Falls and Nisqually Gorge were unsuitable for use as trails as they were too narrow and wet.

From 1880 to 1903, there was a slow but steady influx of new settlers and visitors. The Oscar Allen family arrived near Ashford in 1887. Their homestead is now a Nisqually Land Trust parcel. Three friends each took homesteads on Mineral Creek in 1889 and established Mineral. T.C. Van Eaton established Eatonville in 1889. There was a Hotel Tourist in Elbe sometime around 1890. All of these early settlers had some similar issues. Transportation was slow and awkward—more often packhorses than wagons. Settlers needed to raise food for their families, but their land was covered by trees. This started to change in 1900, as the Tacoma Eastern Railroad announced plans to head into the Cowlitz Valley. As the railway laid out right-of-way plans, the settlers realized that their timberlands had new value. The railroad needed ties, lots of them. Soon, a standard was established. The railroad would pay 5¢ for each tie that was nine feet long, flat on two sides, and within eight feet of the proposed track. Timber harvesting was off and running. With the establishment of Mount Rainier National Park in 1899, even more visitors came. Over the next 100 years, forestry, farming, and tourism became the story of the valley.

There are a few terms we use around here that you might not know the precise definition for: A *stand* of trees is adjoining trees that have one or more common traits, such as species and age: "that stand of cedar by the bridge." *Timber* is standing trees, often a unit of sale: "there is a timber sale today." A *log* is a tree that has had the branches and top removed and what is measured to determine board feet. *Lumber* is what is produced when logs have been cut to a specific size. Rough lumber has not been planed to make it smooth. Green lumber has not been aged or dried in a kiln.

In some of the captions, we have included references to the state highway milepost markers. This will help you compare the historical photograph to the view today:

Alder Cut Off (ACO)
Eatonville Cut Off (ECO)
Highway 7 (Hwy 7)
Highway 161 (Hwy 161)
Highway 706 (Hwy 706)
Mineral Hill Road (MHR)
Mt. Tahoma Canyon (MTC)
Scott-Turner Road (ST)

One

East Branch

The Road to Rainier Scenic Byway's western portal is on State Highway 7 (also called the Mountain Highway or the National Park Highway). Bearing west is State Highway 702, which runs from McKenna to this point. To the east is the Eatonville Cutoff Road. This is the historic community of Leber. Old-timers know this as Rose's Corner, and younger locals know it as the "Yelm Flasher."

The heart of the community was the Weyerhaeuser School. An older structure had been built in 1907 and served the community until the late 1920s when this school was built. Students attended classes have until 1979, when the current school opened two miles to the south.

This class picture from 1943 shows the 27 students of Miss Walter's, who were in the fifth, sixth, seventh, and eighth grades. Another classroom hosted kindergarten and first through fourth grades. Older students were taken by bus to the high school in Eatonville.

Cars are parked around Barneey's Restaurant and Motel at the corner of the Eatonville Cut-Off and State Highway 161. The restaurant had a long history and was something of a roadhouse with dinners, dancing, and drinks. The motel rooms were added in the late 1960s. The motel rooms were converted into apartments in the early 1990s (Hwy 161, milepost 6.1). (Diane Mettler.)

Dogwood Park is just south of the Eatonville Cut-Off on State Highway 161. The park offers a spectacular view of Mount Rainier and was established by the Washington State Department of Transportation and local garden clubs. Signs provide geological information on Mount Rainier and a Blue Star Memorial Highway plaque. The park is now maintained by the Dogwood Garden Club. (Diane Mettler.)

Pictured here are the A.B. Conrad House and family in 1904. The home was on Meridian Avenue, bordering on Northwest Trek. Conrad was a noted photographer of the area. The old East Road (Meridian Avenue) passes in front of the house. Mrs. Conrad is on the left, and A.B. stands next to the third post from the left.

Northwest Trek Wildlife Park is 2.7 miles north of the Eatonville Cut-Off and State Highway 161 junction, on the state highway (Hwy 161, milepost 8.7). The primary attraction is a tram ride tour of the free-range roaming area. The park features animals and habitat native to the Pacific Northwest. A walking tour demonstrates the habitats of birds and smaller animals. Hands-on learning centers allow younger visitors to experience these creatures firsthand.

The Cox Christmas Tree Farm on State Highway 161, just south of Dogwood Park, has been a landmark in the area since 1980. The Christmas tree farm is one of several along the byway. It serves the "U-Cut" family experience seekers. It takes trees 5–10 years to reach market size, and they will be pruned annually to present a full look (Hwy 161, milepost 5.8). (Diane Mettler.)

Fishing was pretty good when this "big one" was landed. The note on the back reads, "The baby you and I got from under the falls on Lynch Creek." Lynch Creek is northeast of Eatonville. The species of trout is unclear; best guess is a steelhead. Steelhead are rainbow trout that run to sea and later return to the river of their birth to mate (Hwy 161, milepost 3.2).

The first school in Eatonville was erected in 1892. In those days, the school year was three months during the summer. The state paid school districts $6 for each student for the three months. The first Eatonville teachers were paid $35 a month. In 1973, it was moved to the Glacier View Park, where it can still be seen.

This second school was completed for classes in 1904. It had two rooms on the first floor and two on the second, plus a small room for an office or library. The second school burned after a fire started in the library in 1909.

The second and third schools were almost identical. The third had two rooms and an office upstairs, three rooms downstairs, and a music room. It had a full basement and a furnace. State funds paid for the minimum required for basic education. The basement typically served as a coatroom and cafeteria. The privy and woodshed were not directly related to education and were funded by either donations or a local bond.

On the Fourth of July in 1915, the community had a parade to mark the laying of a cornerstone for the new high school. The elementary school is on the right. There were now eight classrooms, room for more than 250 students. When the high school opened, it had 49 students enrolled.

The new high school opened in 1916. Serving not only the students of Eatonville but those from all of the communities of southeast Pierce County, the building was progressive, with indoor plumbing, electric lights, and many new technologies and educational spaces. For a time, the Eatonville schools were able to collect a tax on the timber harvest within the school district boundaries. Taxpayers approved but did not pay for the project.

This laboratory room appears to serve many of the sciences. In this posed picture are projects and demonstrations in different fields of study. There are a transit for land surveying, demonstration in seed selection, ant farms, chemistry glassware, and physics appliances as well as posters on animal husbandry.

The home economics room was equipped to teach sewing, nutrition, canning, meal preparation, and etiquette. These students are mixing something, and they have rolling pens at the ready. Some of the workstations have either gas or kerosene burners, and others are electrical.

The pool in the new gymnasium was a source of great pride for the community. The pool and the new gymnasium were built in 1915, the same year as the new high school. Designed not long after the sinking of the *Titanic*, the pool was noted as being the only one in the county, and the school board was very vocal in its desire to have all students learn how to swim.

One of the strongest ties binding all of Eatonville is passion for sports and competition. From the earliest days of the community, there was a baseball team. Seen here is a basketball team from 1916. Over the years, there have been teams that have won state championships and others that have had dismal seasons. It was not a coincidence that in 1915, when the high school was being built, the gymnasium was completed before the academic building was started.

School buses wait to carry students home. One bus would head for the Ohop Valley and Swan Lake, and another went north to Clay City and Kapowsin. The third served the communities of Alder, Elbe, National, and Ashford. The bus coaches were built by the manual training classes and a Mr. Stahler, the instructor. By 1936, the buses were traveling 4,442 miles per month carrying students.

Since 1919, the Eatonville schools have observed Community Day. It started as a thank-you to the community. On the morning of the first Friday of May, the students would go out to the community in service. In the afternoon, the schools invited the community in to thank them. There was singing as well as class presentations and other entertainment. The day concluded with a sporting event, such as track or baseball.

In 1926, the theme of May Day appears to have been adopted by the Community Day. The senior class elected a king and queen, and each of the other classes down to kindergarten elected the queen's court. The entertainment was directed to the court, with the community watching on. Pictured here is the full court from the year 1928.

Another long-term tradition is the maypole dance. The long ribbons held by the students are intertwined around the pole in an intricate pattern determined by the weaving paths of the students. This group is from 1928. The dance is performed after many hours of practice and possibly a few tears of frustration shed by students and teachers alike.

These are some of the patients of the Eatonville Lumberman's Hospital, located on the corner of Lynch Street and Mashell Avenue. In 1908 or 1909 (records differ), Dr. Albert W. Bridge (standing on the left) arrived in town, having ridden his bicycle from Tacoma. He established a clinic at the southwest corner of Washington Avenue and Center Street. Later, he added a second story, providing living accommodations for single nurses.

A large event is taking place here at the corner of Mashell Avenue and Carter Street. Some of the cars have banners proclaiming their participation in some sort of race. The picture also captures a view of the east side of Mashell Avenue. To the right is the boardwalk that links the schools to the commercial district of town.

The Methodist Episcopal church was established in 1903. Over the next nine years, the congregation met in members' homes and other temporary spaces. The congregation bought a partially constructed church building from the Church of Christ and dedicated the structure as its own in 1912. Over the next 100 years, there have been many improvements to the building that kept up with the times while serving the needs of the community.

The double feature this day was Mary Pickford in *A Romance of the Redwoods*, written and directed by Cecil B. DeMille and released in May 1917, and *Sunshine Nan*, starring Ann Pennington and released in 1918. One of the Eatonville seniors recognizes family members and thinks the picture was taken in 1921. This building has been used as a church, office, furniture store, dance studio, and probably for other things.

In a brilliant bit of business planning, the Ice Cream and Confectionery (candy) shop was located close to the schools and theater. Many students could conveniently stop by after school. For an after-theater treat, there were several chairs and tables for the purpose.

The Eatonville Dance Band is a group of local characters—of whom not much is known. Some remember them marching in parades, and they were at some dances. Their uniforms seem to come from the armies of several different countries. The instruments included trumpets, bugles, drums, a baritone, and a saxophone. Two of the members are in blackface, and a third wears a fake hillbilly beard.

The bakery started in the Van Eaton cabin. The cabin was used by several local businesses until they found other accommodations. The bakery moved north across Mashell Avenue to where the Post Net is now. The wood-fired brick oven was in the backyard. This is the bakery as it appeared in 1919. It offered several varieties of breads and rolls, with cakes, pies, and pastries sold by the slice.

Charlie William's Pioneer Garage was a door south of the bakery. Charlie started the garage with funds his father brought home from the Yukon. He had gone north with many others in 1898. He was more fortunate than most, in that he had something to show for his efforts. The purpose-built garage served the family and community well. The vehicle in front belonged to the Eatonville-Tacoma Stage Company.

The Olympia Tavern was located on the south side of the Tall Timbers Cafe. The moveable partitions in the left center were to protect female patrons from having to see the single males on the other side of the partition. This requirement was a part of the laws adopted by the state following the end of Prohibition.

The Order of Redmen Nisqually No. 81 was chartered in 1903 and, by 1904, had constructed a meeting hall. The hall was located at 134 Mashell Avenue. The organization had a strict "white only" membership standard. Like many other organizations of the time, it was a social-gathering place for single men with cut-rate drink prices. Members paid into a burial fund to ensure their funeral expenses would be covered.

The Eatonville Livery & Transfer Stables was two doors north of the barbershop. It rented saddle horses and draft horses for pulling wagons. The draft horses are to the left, and the saddle horses are to the right in this c. 1912 photograph.

This is the interior of the City Barber Shop on Mashell Avenue. This early-1920s picture shows the stand for the electric clippers, the patterned linoleum (not wood) floor, the sign on the mirror showing support for union workers, and the door leading to the bathtubs. The sign leading to the baths proclaims the shop closes at 8:00 p.m. weeknights and at 10:00 p.m. on Saturdays.

The Eatonville Rexall Drugstore was located on the west side of Mashell Avenue, where Kirk's Pharmacy now stands. The building was designed by Dr. Bridge and erected in 1915. The hospital was on the second floor, with a staff of three registered nurses and some nurse's aides. At times, an ambulance was available for transport.

This building was constructed for T.C. Van Eaton around 1895. In its original design, it was 25 feet wide and 100 feet long. The second story was an open room. It was available for rent, and it served the community as a meeting space for nearly 80 years. The ground floor was a grocery store into the 1970s. The site is now a parking lot for a pharmacy.

On the evening of May 7, 1915, a fire broke out on the northeast corner of Mashell Avenue and Center Street. There were four businesses involved: a restaurant, barbershop, hardware store, and saloon. One story says that a drunk and disorderly patron was sent home by the saloon. Upset, he returned, intending to set fire to the saloon. In his sorry state, he set fire to the hardware store by mistake.

C.H. Williamson was an agent for the Bolte & Weyer Lighting System of Chicago, Illinois. Similar in principle to a gas pressurized camping lantern, the system used pressurized gasoline to provide a bright white light. There was a canister on the outside of the cabin holding several quarts of gasoline (lower left and right), a tire pump (lower right) was used to raise the pressure to 50 psi, and tubing (lower center) was used to connect to the burner (lower center right). Burner globes (center left) went over the burner. The white circles are lampshades that fit over the globes. The system was used by homes not connected to electricity. It was popular with circuses and other moving shows. It was not popular with insurance companies.

Popular with the early photographers, the stage vehicles were well photographed. The stage supplemented the trains arriving from Tacoma each day. Records indicate that the first stage may have started in 1912. The earliest motor stage was a White that could carry 12 passengers, with a canvas top and side curtains. There were several companies carrying freight and passengers with different equipment, destinations, and routes.

The rural free delivery driver is loading up for his daily route. It is not known if this shows a daily load or his first day back after a holiday. The sign being held up by the woman at the front of the car proclaims that this is Rural Free Delivery (Route) No. 1, out of Eatonville. The post office was operated out of the Rexall Store for many years.

The first state-chartered bank opened in Eatonville in October 1913. It was located at the southwest corner of Mashell Avenue and Center Street. In 1933, when many banks were failing, the Eatonville bank closed briefly, until the officers presented proof to the auditors that they had sufficient funds to continue operations. In January 1972, the bank became part of Puget Sound National, and in 1993, it was acquired by KeyBank.

This image shows T.C. Van Eaton standing in front of the first building in Eatonville. The cabin, built in 1889, served as both home and store. Over the years, the cabin was used as a "business incubator" as new arrivals set up in the cabin until they went out of business or found or built other accommodations. The building survives in the city's Mill Pond Park.

The hotel was constructed around the first cabin built by Van Eaton. As the hotel building was being demolished in 1997, it was discovered that the first cabin was still in decent condition. The historical society organized the relocation and restoration of the cabin.

This image includes a view of the Eatonville Highway from the early 1930s. The road provided an easy route between Eatonville and the Mountain Highway. In later years, this corridor was heavily used by the Weyerhaeuser Company to move logs from its holdings on the upper Mashel River to the company mill in Vale, Thurston County. Weyerhaeuser had a private railroad and, later, a road system to ease transportation concerns.

The Van Eaton farm was located on the south side of Eatonville Highway. The pond can be seen as one approaches the town limits from the Mountain Highway at the Triangle corner.

In this view looking east on Carter Street in 1980, the Legion Hall is on the right, with the roof of the Van Eaton Chevrolet showroom and the Methodist church to the left. The Van Eaton garage is to the left. Mount Rainier looks down on the scene.

This view looking east on Center Street was taken in 1975, across from the library. On the left is Malcom's Shop-Rite, and on the right are the new city hall and the bank building. On the hills along the upper Mashel River, one can see where harvesting has taken place. Mount Rainier, in the background, watches over the scene.

The town tower was located behind the fire department. Built in 1912, it housed a 34-inch bell that was purchased for $31.50 from the Schabacher Hardware Store. A close-up view indicates that pulleys are attached to the underside of the platform. The proper drying of early canvas hoses was needed to prevent mold and spoilage. The tower collapsed during a December windstorm in 1920 and damaged the Hose House.

The heart of old Eatonville is seen here from the town tower. To the far left is the Van Eaton building. On the east side of Mashell Avenue, one can see the businesses that will be destroyed in the 1915 fire. The large white building (center right) is Dr. Bridge's clinic. Near the bottom on the right is the Eatonville Hotel, with a little corner of the Van Eaton cabin showing under the roof.

The fire department leaders pictured here around 1955 are Ogie Enwall (left); George Smallwood (center), who would later be mayor; and Dick Taylor (right), who is believed to have been the fire chief at the time.

The city hall was built in 1910 to house town government. It had a chamber where the city council and court met, room for clerks, and the town marshal. In the basement were two holding cells. Later, room was found for the clerks of the city utilities. The building was replaced by a greatly expanded facility in 1969.

For many years, the northwest corner of Mashell Avenue and Center Street was occupied by the Van Eaton building. On the ground floor was the Red & White grocery. A true general store, it had a bit of everything. The second story was a large open space. The space was used for almost everything; there were dances, church services, movies, plays, and sporting events. This structure was eventually replaced by a pharmacy's parking lot.

This early photograph of East Center Street was taken around 1896, seven years after the community was founded. Van Eaton's second store is shaded by tall fir trees, and his new home is to the far right. The mother, daughter, and son are pictured just a little east of the first city dug well.

Father, son, and dog bring a log to market in 1902. It is probable they are clearing land on their homestead. Their equipment looks light for commercial logging (the horse is small and the wheels are for medium weights). The first Eatonville sawmill opened in 1898. Selling the log to the sawmill would provide cut lumber or hard-to-find cash. The log scaled at 1,600 board feet.

Hearns Jewelry was located on the southeast corner of Center (Grove) Street and Mashell Avenue. The c. 1914 photograph shows the intersection after the electric power lines were put in. This was a popular location, right at the heart of town. The post office was located in the building from the late 1940s until the late 1970s, when a new post office was built to accommodate the larger mail distribution trucks.

The proprietors and employees of the E.J. Reed tailor shop join their friends from a bathhouse located on East Center Street. This building was built around 1910, before both phone and electric lines. The second floor has living quarters for the business owners or for rent.

The first telephone service in Eatonville was available in 1910; who owned the company at the time and how far one could call are under discussion. The second office was located on the north side of East Center Street, between Mashell and Washington Avenues. For many years, the system provided operator-assisted calls between local residents. It is believed that this building burned down in 1920.

This east-facing view of East Center Street was taken near the bank. There is a gas or kerosene lamp in the intersection; for a time, Eatonville had a lamplighter. The poles are for the telephone wires. The photographer was having a joke as he "renames" the street "Louie" on the negative.

By 1914, several changes have been made. The street has been leveled and covered with gravel. There has been some consideration for storm drains (lower right), The poles on the left side of the street are for electricity. Each pole has a three-phase line for distribution and two lines for the streetlights. Poles on the right are for the telephone company. Every phone subscriber needed his or her own overhead line.

When Dr. Bridge arrived in Eatonville, he opened a clinic here on the southwest corner of Center Street and Washington Avenue. The clinic was on the ground floor, and unmarried nurses had rooms on the second. It was not considered proper for a young lady to live in a boardinghouse. The second floor was removed when the building was sold for other commercial purposes.

The Tacoma Eastern Railroad was the carrier for southern and eastern Pierce County and eastern Lewis County. The business plan was to extract the vast timber resources of the region and ship them to market through Tacoma. The line started construction in 1891 and, after a very slow first 10 years, reached Eatonville in 1903 and Morton in 1908. The line was primarily for freight and was active for 50 years.

The Tacoma Eastern had connections with the Chicago, Milwaukee, St. Paul & Pacific Railroad (the Milwaukee Road). Tacoma Eastern adopted some designs of the Milwaukee Road's rural depots—the bay windows that allowed the stationmaster to view the line in both direction was one. He could do this from both the depot lobby and his living quarters on the second level.

A crowd has gathered in front of the Depot Hotel on the Fourth of July in 1941. The note on the card states that the people are waiting for the 9:30 a.m. train. Old-timers believe the population has gathered to welcome the ball team and fans from another town, who will participate in the parade, games, picnic, and fireworks before they return home in the late evening.

The town has grown, as can be seen from this photograph taken from the lumber mill looking toward the northwest. In foreground, one can see the railroad sidings, the Van Eaton home in the center, the Methodist church to the right, and company houses in the lower left.

This is a c. 1925 view of Eatonville Lumber, taken from the hill southwest of Mashell Avenue and Center Street. The view looks east, with Mashell Avenue at the bottom and company housing in the center and to the right. The large building on the left is the Galbraith home. The mill proper is upper center and to the right. (WSHS 2006.110.1.1.)

The Eatonville Lumber Company was located in the southeast corner of town. The mill itself was between the river and the train tracks. These company houses appear to be on Oak Street. Who lived in which house was regulated by the company according to position and status. The Japanese American quarters were on the far side of the mill, farthest from town.

This is an early view of the mill. Lumber mills produced large amounts of waste wood as they turned round logs into rectangular pieces of lumber. The waste was a problem; left unmanaged, it became a significant fire hazard. The tower was a burner. A conveyor or auger lifted the waste into the burner and dropped it on a slanted grate, with the ash dropping to the floor. The lower level was a water jacket, or a tank built around the fire grate. The water was warmed and then used to feed the steam engines that powered the saws, generators, and other equipment. The top was a spark arrestor to allow the heat and smoke to rise, then allow the wind to blow the smoke away but leave the embers to fall back into the fire.

Large sawmills of the 1930s and 1940s used band saws for most of the length and width cutting of lumber. As the diameter of a log could be in excess of 12 feet, the bands could approach 50 feet in length. Some of the bands have teeth on both sides of the blades; this would allow a cut to be made in both directions. To work efficiently, the saws needed to be kept very sharp. This team of four millwrights is charged with keeping the bands sharp and in working order. There are approximately 10 saw bands on the floor and more in the rafters. The millwrights were expected to be able to change out the bands while the crew was at lunch.

The Eatonville Lumber Company baseball team gathers for a team photograph on April 26, 1927. The size of the grandstands is for multiple thousands of fans, so it must be in Tacoma, Seattle, or Portland. All of the team members are of Japanese ancestry. The umpire and another man standing in the second row are Caucasian. (WSHS 1957.64.D1719.)

Family and friends of the Sakura family gather in Eatonville. All are enjoying what appears to be a pleasant summer afternoon. This photograph, taken during the Depression, conveys no sense of the desperation that is depicted in other images captured during that time. David Sakura adds that it shows that one can be happy while living in " 'company housing,' an outlook on life that is in keeping with my father, Chester, 'sunny' disposition." (Sakura family.)

Built as a springhouse for the Eatonville Lumber Company dairy, this building was converted to a farm shed when the dairy closed. The women of the Japanese American community then adapted it to serve as a production center for tofu. The historical society is working to restore the building, one of the last artifacts of the Japanese American community in the valley, and use it for an exhibition on the contributions of the Japanese Americans.

The men who actually cut the trees down were called fallers. They were highly skilled and very fit as they used saws, axes, hammers and wedges for each tree. Here, a filer is working on a 6-to-8-foot saw in an adjustable saw vice. Each faller needed a least two saws—preferably four. The saws needed to be sharpened after a day's use and customized for each person. The filer could adjust the set, bite, and pitch for each tooth to match the type of timber being harvested and the preferences of the faller. This shop was a modified railcar that followed the movement of the logging camps.

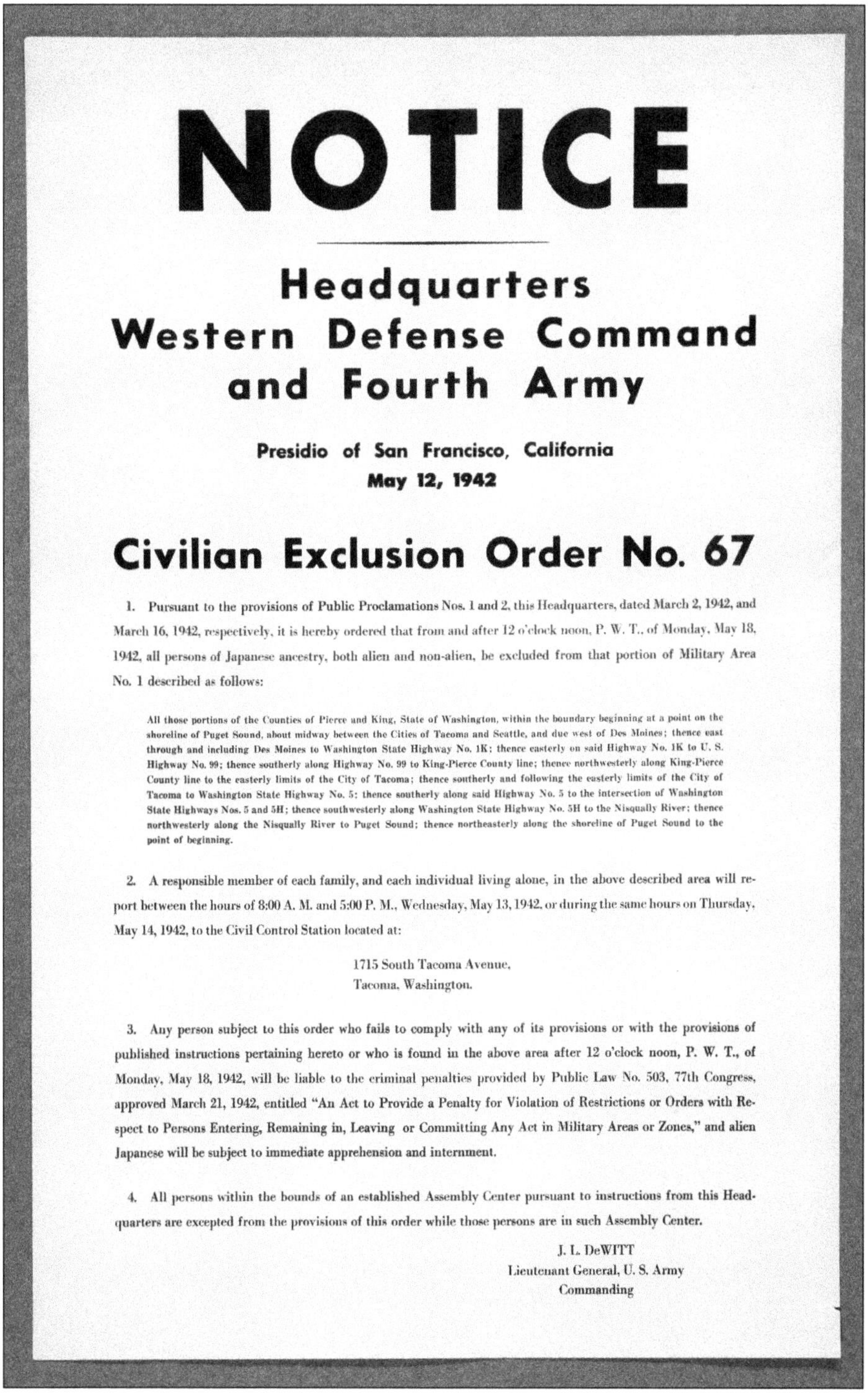
NOTICE

Headquarters Western Defense Command and Fourth Army

Presidio of San Francisco, California
May 12, 1942

Civilian Exclusion Order No. 67

1. Pursuant to the provisions of Public Proclamations Nos. 1 and 2, this Headquarters, dated March 2, 1942, and March 16, 1942, respectively, it is hereby ordered that from and after 12 o'clock noon, P. W. T., of Monday, May 18, 1942, all persons of Japanese ancestry, both alien and non-alien, be excluded from that portion of Military Area No. 1 described as follows:

All those portions of the Counties of Pierce and King, State of Washington, within the boundary beginning at a point on the shoreline of Puget Sound, about midway between the Cities of Tacoma and Seattle, and due west of Des Moines; thence east through and including Des Moines to Washington State Highway No. 1K; thence easterly on said Highway No. 1K to U. S. Highway No. 99; thence southerly along Highway No. 99 to King-Pierce County line; thence northwesterly along King-Pierce County line to the easterly limits of the City of Tacoma; thence southerly and following the easterly limits of the City of Tacoma to Washington State Highway No. 5; thence southerly along said Highway No. 5 to the intersection of Washington State Highways Nos. 5 and 5H; thence southwesterly along Washington State Highway No. 5H to the Nisqually River; thence northwesterly along the Nisqually River to Puget Sound; thence northeasterly along the shoreline of Puget Sound to the point of beginning.

2. A responsible member of each family, and each individual living alone, in the above described area will report between the hours of 8:00 A. M. and 5:00 P. M., Wednesday, May 13, 1942, or during the same hours on Thursday, May 14, 1942, to the Civil Control Station located at:

1715 South Tacoma Avenue,
Tacoma, Washington.

3. Any person subject to this order who fails to comply with any of its provisions or with the provisions of published instructions pertaining hereto or who is found in the above area after 12 o'clock noon, P. W. T., of Monday, May 18, 1942, will be liable to the criminal penalties provided by Public Law No. 503, 77th Congress, approved March 21, 1942, entitled "An Act to Provide a Penalty for Violation of Restrictions or Orders with Respect to Persons Entering, Remaining in, Leaving or Committing Any Act in Military Areas or Zones," and alien Japanese will be subject to immediate apprehension and internment.

4. All persons within the bounds of an established Assembly Center pursuant to instructions from this Headquarters are excepted from the provisions of this order while those persons are in such Assembly Center.

J. L. DeWITT
Lieutenant General, U. S. Army
Commanding

This is a notice that "all persons of Japanese ancestry, both alien and non-alien, be excluded from that portion of Military Area N. 1." It was given to thousands, announcing that they had two days to report to military authorities and six days to permanently leave the western portions of Pierce County and southwest King County during World War II. (WSHS 1993.16.2.)

This 1895 photograph was taken of six friends at the Mashel River. This is an early bridge and not one designed for heavy loads. The bridge was suitable for horses, packtrains, farm carts, and light coaches. The logs that span the river could only hold several tons. (WSHS 2017.0.45.)

This bridge also spans the Mashel River but is designed to be much stronger than the 1895 bridge. The abutments that support the trusses are of stone and masonry and are well built. The beams are larger, and there is more iron with both tie-rods and cables used to distribute weight and add strength. The built-in guardrails work to protect the bridge from accidents.

There are three bridge crossings of the Mashel River: one southeast of Eatonville on the Alder Cut-Off Road, one south on Mashell Avenue, and another on the Mountain Highway. Telling one bridge from another is difficult. The bridges are each approximately 80 feet long and 20 feet wide. There is no clear view of the foundation, but most bridges of this kind were built on two or three logs that spanned the opening, and then the wooden deck and superstructure were added. The later bridges were built to carry the weight of heavy loads of logs.

The first wagon road from Eatonville to Elbe was built in 1895 and is seen here in an 1896 photograph taken by Alvin Waite on his way to Mount Rainier. The corduroy road was nine miles long and cost Pierce County $18,000. A county surveyor noted about the road "that grades were high (34%), subject to snow closures as it passed over Mashel Mountain, three feet of soft mud, slides and floods."

The grade on the Alder Cut-Off Road from the Mashell Bridge to the Scott-Turner Road is often under repair. The road was realigned to accommodate the rerouting of the railroad when Tacoma Public Utilities built the new dams on the Nisqually. (TPU 13339.)

The fill on which the road is built keeps sloughing away. Unbeknownst to the construction crew, a portion of the road was built over an undiscovered spring, causing portions of the roadway to be displaced. A number of corrections have been attempted, but the least expensive and most effective is to lay a new asphalt patch. Here, a road engineer from the City of Tacoma contemplates what action to recommend. It took the city over 30 years of work before it could transfer the road to the county. A local question is, How many feet of asphalt are in the patches? (TPU 13963.)

Students from Columbia Crest School in cooperation with the Nisqually River Foundation participate in a fish toss on the upper reaches of the Mashel River (ACO, milepost 4.3). Researchers discovered that salmon rivers need nutrients found in salmon carcasses to help salmon smolt thrive. The students have fun getting wet and smelly. (Nisqually River Foundation.)

Following the Scott-Turner Road, the road passes the entrance to the Elbe Hills State Forest on its way to Ashford. A state Discover Pass is required for entry to this area. The reward for taking this route is a series of great views of Mount Rainier. The patchy look of the hillside is due to timber harvesting. Stands of trees mature at different times, depending on soil, sun orientation, drainage, and altitude.

A little volunteer joins his family and others from the community at the annual fish toss. Though it is not as famous as the one at Seattle's Pike Place Market, it can still be fun. The family is at Eatonville's Smallwood Park on the Mashel River. Behind the group is a children's fishpond stocked so that children can try and catch their own dinners. (Nisqually River Foundation.)

The Alder Lake Stump Forest is left over from the construction of the Alder and La Grande Dams in the early 1940s. When the reservoir was laid out, the timber was harvested to defray some of the cost of construction. There was no value in removing the stumps. The seasonal filling and draining of the reservoir delays decomposition. It is now more than 75 years since the land was cleared.

Two

West Branch

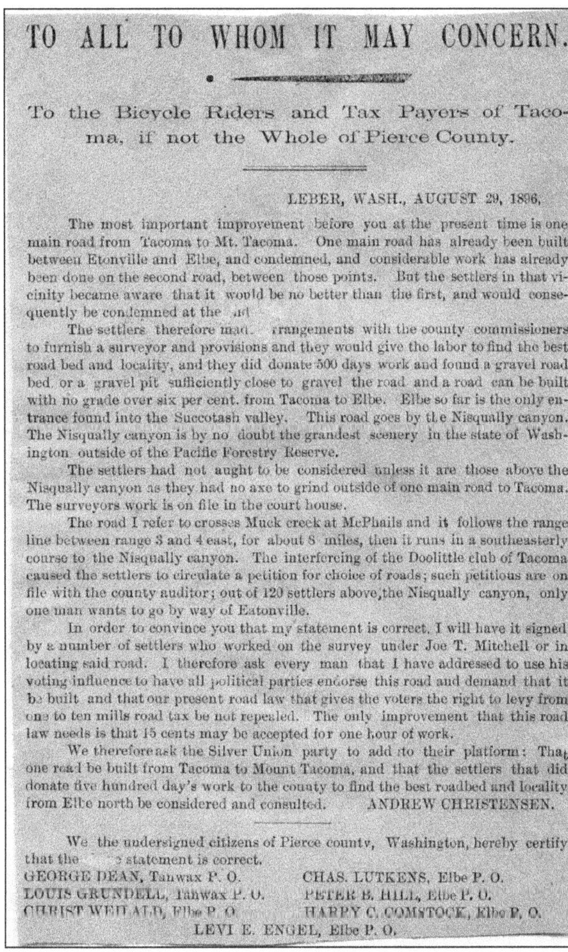

TO ALL TO WHOM IT MAY CONCERN.

To the Bicycle Riders and Tax Payers of Tacoma, if not the Whole of Pierce County.

LEBER, WASH., AUGUST 29, 1896.

The most important improvement before you at the present time is one main road from Tacoma to Mt. Tacoma. One main road has already been built between Etonville and Elbe, and condemned, and considerable work has already been done on the second road, between those points. But the settlers in that vicinity became aware that it would be no better than the first, and would consequently be condemned at the [illegible]

The settlers therefore mad[illegible] [illegible]rangements with the county commissioners to furnish a surveyor and provisions and they would give the labor to find the best road bed and locality, and they did donate 500 days work and found a gravel road bed or a gravel pit sufficiently close to gravel the road and a road can be built with no grade over six per cent. from Tacoma to Elbe. Elbe so far is the only entrance found into the Succotash valley. This road goes by the Nisqually canyon. The Nisqually canyon is by no doubt the grandest scenery in the state of Washington outside of the Pacific Forestry Reserve.

The settlers had not aught to be considered unless it are those above the Nisqually canyon as they had no axe to grind outside of one main road to Tacoma. The surveyors work is on file in the court house.

The road I refer to crosses Muck creek at McPhails and it follows the range line between range 3 and 4 east, for about 8 miles, then it runs in a southeasterly course to the Nisqually canyon. The interfercing of the Doolittle club of Tacoma caused the settlers to circulate a petition for choice of roads; such petitious are on file with the county auditor; out of 120 settlers above, the Nisqually canyon, only one man wants to go by way of Eatonville.

In order to convince you that my statement is correct, I will have it signed by a number of settlers who worked on the survey under Joe T. Mitchell or in locating said road. I therefore ask every man that I have addressed to use his voting influence to have all political parties endorse this road and demand that it be built and that our present road law that gives the voters the right to levy from one to ten mills road tax be not repealed. The only improvement that this road law needs is that 15 cents may be accepted for one hour of work.

We therefore ask the Silver Union party to add to their platform: That one road be built from Tacoma to Mount Tacoma, and that the settlers that did donate five hundred day's work to the county to find the best roadbed and locality from Elbe north be considered and consulted. ANDREW CHRISTENSEN.

We the undersigned citizens of Pierce county, Washington, hereby certify that the [illegible] statement is correct.

GEORGE DEAN, Tanwax P. O. — CHAS. LUTKENS, Elbe P. O.
LOUIS GRUNDELL, Tanwax P. O. — PETER B. HILL, Elbe P. O.
CHRIST WEHALD, Elbe P. O. — HARRY C. COMSTOCK, Elbe P. O.
LEVI E. ENGEL, Elbe P. O.

The need to improve the transportation between the population centers on Puget Sound and the wonders of Mount Rainier was of great importance to the citizens of the Nisqually Valley in 1896. Leber resident Andrew Christensen issued a call to the "Bicycle Riders and Tax Payers of Tacoma." He reported that only one of the 120 landholders in the valley preferred the Mashel Mountain Road over the Nisqually Canyon route that he and his neighbors had built. Christensen appealed to bicyclists for support as they were the largest group using the route. (WSHS 1903.1.168.)

In the late 1890s, bicycling was fast becoming a popular form of transportation, with the number of cyclists growing each year. Women joined the craze, attending classes and wearing baggy pants called bloomers as they cycled the growing network of trails. Cycling clubs sprang up in many communities. The clubs wanted better bike trails that went somewhere members wanted to go and were not muddy in the winter and dusty in the summer. (MOHAI Shs_13467.)

Roscoe and Lottie King opened a small roadside business at the top of Ohop Hill in the early 1920s. The business was popular and supported a number of families over the years. It started by offering fuel, tire service, and a garage. Later, a lunch counter was added, and locals started dropping by for breakfast and coffee. During World War II, times were tough, as tourists were unable to come due to gas and rubber rationing. Locals, loggers, truckers, and the men building the new dams helped keep things going. After the war, the tourists returned in greater numbers. But by the late 1960s, road conditions and car reliability had improved so that tourists did not need to stop at roadside businesses. Business declined, and by the early 1970s, the then owners, a Mr. and Mrs. Dolman, had the old building burned down.

A group of young adults takes a break and has a picnic on its way to Mount Rainier. The photograph shows the people between Leber and Ohop. A note on the back states that it was taken in 1917. The car on the right appears to be a 1916 Scripps Booth. The middle car is a Ford Model T, and the car on the right might be a 1915 Dodge. (WSDOT Dads.)

Ohop Bob was a favorite eatery on the route to Mount Rainier. Located halfway between Tacoma and Paradise Valley, it offered a variety of cuisine, with southern fried chicken being a favorite. Many families put off stopping until the return trip, as it could take several hours to complete the meal, and if they stopped on the way up, they may lose the chance to play at Mount Rainier. (Jean Shields.)

When Torger Petersen viewed the Ohop Valley in 1887, he found a slow-draining wetland that stretched from Clay City to the Nisqually River. There was not a single channel, but a network of shallow ponds. This might be natural, but it was not good for a dairy farmer seeking pastureland.

The Ohop Valley is seen here; after a portion of the headwaters had been diverted, Ohop Lake was created by construction of a dam. A deep-sided main channel was dug, with many laterals draining the edges of the wetland into the main canal. Salmon found insufficient pools to allow a return to their spawning grounds.

Scientists have learned that this work harmed the habitat of salmon runs that used the creek for spawning. The Nisqually Land Trust, Nisqually River Council, Nisqually Tribe, students from Columbia Crest and other schools, and various partners have been working to restore the creek to vitality. They have removed the channel, slowed the flow, planted trees to provide shade and promote a spawning environment. (Nisqually River Foundation.)

The Ohop Ladies Aid Society met in 1909 to card wool for knitting. Most of the Ohop residents were from Norway. The society worked to help the families learn English, conducted citizenship classes, supported the local school, and, in general, enabled better citizens and strengthened the community.

Pioneer Farms is a local educational outreach that allows visitors to view the kinds of facilities the pioneer forefathers used. A number of pioneer-era buildings were moved to the site to create a model farm, which includes a farmhouse, school, barn, and smithy. Visitors are given demonstrations and then a chance to learn for themselves how much it effort takes to cut firewood, carry water, or operate the bellows at the forge.

Younger visitors to Pioneer Farm enjoy the experience of touching the barnyard animals. Here, one young visitor gets to ride the farm's horse. During his visit, he also milked the cow, picked up a chicken, and rubbed the tummy of a pig. The farm also has a hayloft and a slide.

The Ohop settlers were very civic minded. In Washington, all males had to work two days a year or pay $4 to vote. The settlers observed that the influx of tourists was creating a demand for milk, butter, meats, and produce. To transport their crops to the new market, they needed a road with easy access to Mount Rainier. They worked together to build a road through the Nisqually Canyon.

Washing laundry was a major chore for pioneer women, and it could take a whole day to finish a family's wash. At right, Hanna Olden has her water on the stove heating, and the washboard is in the wash pan. She will wet the clothes, use a bar of soap, scrub on the washboard, rinse several times, and then wring the item by hand. She hangs it on the line until the sun and wind have dried it. Below, Maren Christenson has taken a different approach. Her home has electricity, and the family has ordered a Thor washing machine from Chicago. She uses a hose to fill the machine, which will then agitate the clothes to separate the dirt from the laundry. She is using the power wringer to force out the water. The used water drains from the valve on the bottom of the machine.

According to South Sound Prairies, a local conservation group, the byway passes through historic prairies. These open savannas were created by retreating glaciers at the end of the Ice Age. The pioneers reported that there were grasslands in the lower Ohop, on the Swan Lake Plateau, and along the Stringtown Road. Unlike the rich soil of the Midwest plains, these plains have gravelly soils that dried out quickly during summer heat. Native Americans sustained these grassy plains for thousands of years, using fire to keep the encroaching forests at bay. Today, prescribed burning is used by land managers for a variety of reasons. One benefit of contained burning is to maintain the health of an existing natural area containing native plants. The fire helps manage weeds and other growth, thus helping to reduce the risk of wildfires. However, fire also helps restore nutrients and leads to more desirable plant growth in the future. (South Sound Prairies 001,002.)

The Tacoma Eastern pioneers recalled the salmon bakes at which the Indian Henry family periodically entertained their friends and neighbors. The pioneer would arrive in a wagon. The Henry family would provide the salmon, baked over fires in the ground. The neighbors would provide all the rest of the food. The Henry family loved pickles and cheese. All enjoyed the huckleberry cobbler.

Charles Lathrop Pack Demonstration Forest was a gift to the University of Washington from Pack. He grew up in the upper Midwest, where unrestrained logging had not only destroyed the forest but also left behind thousands of acres of dead land. Pack wanted to have a location for the scientific study of forest management. His vision has resulted in a 4,200-acre forest laboratory that offers hiking trails open to the public.

The forest continues to be a part of the university and some research continues, but the lessons for forest sustainability have been learned and applied. The Rainier Institute has taken up residence and continues teaching new generations the need for better understanding of environmental interactions. (UofW Pack Forest.)

From 1912 to 1926, the American Nitrogen Company was a major presence in La Grande. Using the low-cost electricity from the dam, the plant pioneered the process for removing nitrogen from the air and making nitrate of soda crystals for explosives and fertilizer. The potential for chemical release, fire, or explosion was understood. Employees were encouraged to live away from the plant. There was never a school at La Grande.

Gilbert's store was built in 1910 on the edges of the City of Tacoma and Tacoma Eastern properties. It served the workers building the project and housed the post office for the area. The "Z" turns in La Grande were designed to have road traffic cross the railroad tracks at right angles. (Loren Lane.)

The Canyada Lodge was built on the grounds of an earlier commercial picnic area in 1912. There was a swing bridge across the canyon that gave access to a trail system, an archery range, and other amusements. The lodge was about halfway between Tacoma and Longmire Springs. It was there for those who needed to take two days for the trip. The lodge burned in 1926.

The Ohop farmer's road through the Nisqually Canyon allowed people and freight to reach the settlement at Longmire one day faster. The farmers struck a bargain with the county to donate 500 hours of labor if the county would provide gravel for the new road. (UofW WAT084.)

In 1909, Tacoma voted to have its own utility company. The city set out to construct a hydroelectric dam on the Nisqually River. The first dam was completed in 1910. The dam seen in the center was designed to divert some of the water into a canal (on the right) that carried a portion of the river into a system of canals and tunnels to the powerhouse three miles downriver.

The Nisqually Project had two tunnels, each about a mile long. Here, a crew of Welsh miners starts at one end. There were four crews—one for each portal. After this project was completed, some of the miners moved on to work the coal mine at Ladd near Mineral. (TPU 42897*54.)

The penstocks at the La Grande powerhouse are 5 feet wide and drop the water 410 feet. The powerhouse and the penstocks are the ones that were built in 1910. In 1938–1944, there were modifications that installed four sets of Allis-Chalmers turbines and generators each producing 8,000 horsepower. The first phase of the project was completed exactly as specified, on time, and on budget. (TPL D8266.)

The construction of the first transmission line from La Grande to the substation in Tacoma was a major project in itself. It was work within the capabilities of local companies. The land had to be cleared of trees, timber, and brush. A service road had to be built to allow for line and right-of-way maintenance. Poles were set to carry the lines. The stringing of the lines was done by specialists.

By the late 1920s, it was becoming apparent that Tacoma needed additional power to support its growing industries. Planning started but was delayed by the Depression. This second phase included the building of two new dams and powerhouses and the creation of Alder Lake as a reservoir. World War II slowed the completion of the project.

In the 1950s, Tacoma City Light started the development of recreation facilities around the lake. This site was chosen as the location for a camping and picnicking park named Alder Park. Over the years, a boat launch, swim area, and RV and group camping have been added. (TPU 7891.)

This view of Mount Rainier was offshore the Sunny Point Swim Area. Mount Rainier is a 14,411-foot stratovolcano. The mountain rises abruptly from the surrounding land. There are 23 named glaciers and numerous unnamed snowfields. From this view, the Tahoma, South Tahoma, Kautz,

Van Trump, Wilson, and Nisqually glaciers are visible. The mountain has a number of sensors to monitor seismic activity so researchers can learn more about volcanoes. There is continuing research into the advance and retreat of the glaciers correlating to changes in climate. (TPU 64.)

The falls on the Nisqually at La Grande prevent fish from going up or down to the ocean. However, the lakes and stream above the falls did have an abundance of fish, according to the pioneers. Sportfishing groups and the Washington State Department of Fish and Wildlife stock many lakes and streams in the area with species like rainbow trout. This young lady would probably like to land one. (TPU Little Fisher.)

The Reliance Mill in Alder is seen here in 1910. The mill was located near the current Lilie Dale peninsula. There were several mills on the Nisqually River upriver from the Tacoma City Dam. They were rather small, using the river for millponds and having sidings on the Tacoma Eastern for getting the lumber to market. The mills joined together to build a hydroelectric dam several years before Tacoma. (WSHS 1943.42.191.1.)

Alder was always more of a logging and farming community than a tourist town. Settlers came after the railroads had reached Ashford, the destination for most park visitors. The townsite was flooded by the new reservoir; only five buildings were moved to higher ground. (TPU 6854.)

Boaters have found much to do on Alter Lake. The knowledgeable boater can explore the remains of Old Alder, Reliance, and a train trestle when water levels are right. There are many miles of lakeshore to explore, and some enjoy the water-skiing. (TPU 17012.)

Alder was one of the areas in the valley where larger farms prospered. Before the basin was flooded, there were field crops and orchards. Lucky homesteaders were able to file for land that had both trees and open ground. The trees could be harvested and sold for cash. The stumps had to be removed to have an efficient farm. This young couple was caught looking grimy by the camera.

On March 18, 1939, people living near Alder, looked up to see this Boeing 307 Stratoliner fall to earth. The four-engine aircraft, designed to revolutionize cross-country transportation was the first pressurized passenger plane. The plane broke apart as it fell and crashed into the Nisqually Valley. All 10 men aboard died on impact. The airframe was reworked for the Army Air Forces as a heavy bomber designated as the B-17. (TPL D8032_2.)

Three

South Branch

The churches in Elbe were built at the same time in 1906 to serve the community. The number of German-speaking Lutherans was fewer than the number of English-speaking Presbyterians, so the Lutheran church was built smaller. Services were conducted in German until America's entry into World War I. The cemetery for both Elbe and Ashford was between the church and the river. When the lake was formed, the remains were moved.

The Forestry Building was erected in 1936 by a public works program to provide a base for the fire crews hired by private forest landowners. In this August 1937 photograph, the second story was used as quarters and offices for the seasonal crews. The ground floor had a garage for the pumper truck and storage and shop space for tools and equipment. The building is now a public rest area. (WSHS 1950_1301 _22_11.)

Berlin was the major cross street in Old Elbe. This view of the identified businesses on the east side of the street include Greaves Barber Shop, the Carter's Elbe Hotel, and Reber Grocery. The high boardwalk and muddy street must have made crossing the street difficult.

The Mount Rainier Scenic Railroad had humble beginnings. Tom Murray Jr. had grown up living around steam engines and steam-powered logging equipment. In the early 1980s, he sponsored the restoration of a collection of geared logging locomotives. He then started offering rides from Elbe to Mineral Lake. Seen here are passengers waiting to board the first train. (Tim Hale.)

The second Hotel Tourist was built by Henry and Charles Luckin in 1894; it was a log building with a distinctive veranda on the Nisqually River side with chairs where tourist could sit and enjoy the view. The hotel was a popular stop, as it was a day's travel from both Eatonville and Longmire Springs.

The first community in the upper Nisqually valley, Elbe is located at one of the few places along the river that is bridgeable. The river is narrowed by rock outcrops, and a long log can be placed across the waterway. This may be one of the first bridges. It is roughly made of logs with split-log decking. Later bridges used milled lumber.

Levi Engle came from Pilger, Nebraska, as a homesteader in 1889 at age 19. He was the enterprising sort and soon had the homestead going; he then became the editor of the *Elbe Union*. An intuitive mechanic, he soon had freight wagons and a blacksmith shop. He added a gas drum and his first customer was Pres. William Howard Taft, making a trip to Mount Rainier. This is a self-portrait.

Yes, that is a giraffe—when one first sees Dan Klennert's Recycled Spirits of Iron Sculpture Park, one may wonder. Ex-Nihilo Park (from the Latin for "something created from nothing") is a different experience. All the expressions were wrought from the imagination and materials found by the artist.

From forty feet, this looks like a seahorse. This closer look exposes the artistic imagination used to form the sculpture. The scales are used horseshoes. The chest is a wheel from a conveyer system. The crest is some form of cutting wheel. The sculpture park is free, with easy parking. The idea is to roam to where something has caught one's attention. There are many jokes and puns among the different sculptures.

The fields at Park Junction are the remains of early ranching. The name indicates that near here, the Tacoma Eastern Railroad's tracks split, with a spur going on to Ashford while the main line continued across the Nisqually and down to Morton. During winter months, the fields supports a herd of elk. The fields offer the traveler a good view of the top of Mount Rainier in clear weather. (Loren Lane.)

Students from the Columbia Crest School in Ashford work with students from Evergreen State College and the Nisqually River Foundation to conduct an annual invertebrate inventory to document the health of the Nisqually River near their school. It is hoped that data collected over many years will help researchers better understand the riverine environment. (Nisqually River Foundation.)

North of the road, five miles east of Elbe, is the Sahara Creek DNR Horse Camp. Developed for the use of backcountry horsemen, the campground provides two- and four-legged visitors with access to 40 miles of the Nicholson Horse Trail system. The trails use orphaned logging roads and railbeds to pass by historical logging sites to reach higher elevations with views of the surrounding mountains. A Discover Pass is required for access. (Nancy Barker.)

Horse trails require some different maintenance standards than other trails. Greater height clearance is required, as are greater widths and some places for stopping and passing. Bridges and boardwalks need to be more than 10 times stronger than for humans. Volunteers do much of the maintenance work in the roadless area themselves. Here, a pack train carries replacement parts for a damaged bridge. (Nancy Barker.)

Back Country Horsemen groups have worked with the Department of Natural Resources to make part of the Elbe Hills State Forest horse friendly. Over the years, these volunteers have helped to build an overnight camping area with hitching rails, trailer loading and parking area, water troughs, and other amenities to improve the care of livestock. (Nancy Barker.)

The Elbe Hills State Forest has a portion of the forest dedicated to the mutual use of off-highway/road vehicle groups and individuals. Volunteers from the Pacific Northwest Four Wheel Drive Association and other groups have developed challenges specific for their sport. Here, a vehicle passes over the "log crawl" installed in cooperation with the Department of Natural Resources. (Nancy Barker.)

The National Mill was highly dependent on the railroad for receiving logs and shipping lumber. This Pacific National's Heisler locomotive No. 4 pulls a string of cars to the log dump. Just in front of the cab of the engine, a part of the gear-drive system is visible. Logging railroads were required to take tighter corners and to climb higher than normal grades. This picture is from 1924. (WSHS 1957.64.B9902.)

This load of mixed fir and cedar logs is being shunted onto a siding after leaving a landing, where the logs were placed on the flatcars. This train is local, from a siding to a mill or "reload." Since 1916, log cars have not been allowed on main or intercity tracks unless the logs were chained or binders were used to keep them from shifting. (WSHS 1957.64.B9903.)

An unusual feature of the National Mill was the ability to move and cut very long logs. Most logs or lumber were limited to 40 feet. The trolley that carried the logs past the main ripsaw (headrig) moved on tracks over 130 feet long. There was a lucrative market for long logs and lumber. They were used for ship's keels, masts and rigging, and utility poles. Logs that had been trimmed to make them square were called cants. (WSHS 1957.64.B9900.)

The method for transporting oversized logs or lumber was to use three flatcars. The units were loaded onto the middle car and bound to that car. Each end had a frame built around it, so all of the ends moved as one. As the train rounded a curve, the ends of the units could sweep across the end cars but would continue to be straight. In this picture, the sweep motion has been limited. Great care had to be taken on double-track lines to make sure there was no oncoming traffic on curves. The Tacoma Eastern Railroad was ideal for moving these loads; the line did not have sharp curves, and all trains were controlled by the same office from mill to dockside. (WSHS 1957.64.B9899.)

From the 1890s to the late 1950s, many employers sponsored baseball teams. The National Loggers was a team from Ashford. The team was sometimes sponsored by the Weyerhaeuser Company. Pictured are team members (first row) Frank Bloom, Frank Lyday, Don Fore, Don Rose and Jack Chappel; (second row) Don Stewart, Mel Ceccanti, Al Mierke, Bob Fore, and Jack Lyday. (Marie Fore estate.)

This crew of men of Japanese ancestry was the track crew for the Pacific National operations in National. Some of the younger men were American-born citizens, and most of the others gained citizenship through naturalization. The track crew removed unneeded lines and then constructed new rail lines as the logging operations moved to new areas. (Rick Johnson and Ashford Creek Pottery.)

The Mount Tahoma Trail Association maintains cabins and cross-country and snowshoe trails on both sides of Highway 706. The roads to use are marked on the highway. The trails follow active and orphaned logging routes deep into the Central Cascade foothills. These are the areas logged for the Pacific National mill and replanted. Cabin space can be scheduled by contacting the association in Ashford. (Washington State Department of Natural Resources.)

A family using one of the Mount Tahoma Trail Association trails crosses an intersecting trail left over from prior logging operations (Hwy 701, milepost 6.2). The trees were planted in a forest recovery effort by the Department of Natural Resources and will soon be ready for harvesting. State forests are an important source of revenue for state institutions. (Washington State Department of Natural Resources.)

Snowmobiles are seldom seen in the lower elevations of the Nisqually Valley. On rare occasions, they may be seen supporting the trails of the Mount Tahoma Trail Association. Their natural range is above 3,500 feet in altitude, which includes the roads of upper Copper Creek, Osborn Mountain, and the area around Highrock.

On April 27, 1915, the Tacoma Publicity Committee sponsored a race from Tacoma to Mount Rainier (Ashford), pitting a train against four automobiles. The train was a Milwaukee Road Special, handled by engineer A.W. Bagley and conductor J.F. Beals. The train arrived five minutes before the leading vehicle, driven by Mrs. O.H. Ridgeway (in car No. 2) at a blistering speed of 40–50 miles per hour. (TPL-1039.)

Motor buses and other vehicles collect passengers from the Tacoma Eastern depot in Ashford. They will take the visitors to hotels at Longmire Springs. Some will move on to adventures at Paradise Valley, Camp in the Clouds, and Indian Henry's Hunting Grounds. This Asahel Curtis photograph was taken around 1910. (WSHS 1943.42.19417.)

Edmond S. Meany was a famed historian, Mount Rainier researcher, and the father of the University of Washington forestry school. He led a number of scientific expeditions to Mount Rainier to research topics such as botany, geology, glaciers, and volcanology. He served as president of the Seattle Mountaineers from 1908 to 1937. Here, President Meany drives a motor bus from Ashford. (WSHS 1999.120.1.78.)

This view of Mount Rainier is at the end of Cooper Creek Road or Forest Service Road No. 59. This is a primitive forest service road and subject to frequent flooding. The first several hundred yards are bumpy. Once the traveler leaves the valley floor, he or she soon starts climbing the side of the valley. The road ends at trailheads for Mount Wow and the Glacier View Wilderness. (Loren Lane.)

A parade of tour buses winds its way on the road between Ashford and Longmire Springs around 1912. Note how the road moves around the trees. The large trees were left standing until new technology would allow profitable harvesting. (UofW WAS0612.)

In 1915, this group of over 150 mountaineers gathered at the depot in Ashford. They had started in Seattle and transferred in Tacoma to reach Ashford. Here, they begin a three-week adventure to hike around the mountain, establishing camping sites and improving the Wonderland Trail. This was the first time any group or individual had completed the full circuit. (WSHS 1999.120.1.1.)

In 1911, Stephen Mather, the father of the National Park System, requested all national parks erect "an archway of rustic design at the entrance to the Park." He felt that this would help the visitors understand that they were entering somewhere special. The tradition has been continued, and most national parks follow the suggestion. At Mount Rainier, the gate was built in 1911 and replaced in 1972 (Hwy 706, milepost 14.6).

Four

MINERAL BRANCH

Milwaukee Road engine No. 1277 pulls a load of cars across the trestle, through a covered bridge, and over the Nisqually River between Park Junction in Pierce County and Flynn in Lewis County. Covered bridges were erected where heavy snows might accumulate over water. The bridges needed to be tall to accommodate tall loads and have a means for dispersing smoke and steam. This photograph was taken in 1941. (WSHS 2012_74_68.)

This is a view of the Flynn Mill and Mineral Creek at the end of Flynn Road. Logs to be cut are in the lower left. The mill is to the lower right. There is no millpond, and it appears that the logs are moved by cable or brute force. The J.D. Hale homestead consists of the buildings at left center. The mill was dismantled by the summer of 1934. (Jim Hale.)

Richard Loden homesteaded near Mineral in 1891. His property included where the creek from Mineral Lake joins Mineral Creek. Like many of his Scandinavian neighbors, he soon cleared enough land to have a few cows. This barn is one of the oldest in the area still standing and was built using split cedar planking. (Katelyn Holmes.)

The barn is now the home for a 1928 Chevrolet/Ford (mix) one-and-a-half-ton truck used to help with the chores on the farm and for trips to town. The current owner contends that with "just a little work" and new tires, the truck would be ready to run again. "It worked when we parked it," he explains. (Katelyn Holmes.)

A family moved onto one of the original homesteads of Mineral. Over the years, they have recovered these items from barns and sheds, trash pits, and other sites around the property. This wall displays over 125 years of technology used around this home.

After a successful career in Seattle, Jim Hale moved back to Mineral for his retirement. He bought a disused farm closer to the Mineral village and set to work planting and trimming Christmas trees. For over 30 years, he and his family helped others enjoy a traditional holiday. (Jim Hale.)

For many years, the tradition for Mineral students was to end the school year with a picnic and games. This particular year, students and mothers have gathered at the Mineral Creek Bridge for the games. In this image, it appears the mothers are having a race—there is no word on who won. (Jim Hale.)

The Tacoma Eastern Railroad arrived in Mineral in September 1905. The depot was completed in 1906. With its telegraph connections, it controlled train traffic for the mills, mines, and loggers in the area. It took four additional years for the tracks to reach Morton. The depot was an agent for Wells Fargo and delivered freight to the locals. This photograph was taken on Christmas Day 1908.

Richard Loden hunted extensively in the area and soon became aware of a very large tree. When the railroad arrived, the tracks were close to what became known as the "Exhibition Tree." When the Tacoma Eastern Railroad passenger trains reached Mineral, they sometimes stopped to let travelers walk the short distance so they could carve their names into the bark. The tree was nearly 14 feet in circumference, 200 feet high, and some 1,200 years old.

This eight-car train was needed to move the "Exhibition Tree" to a mill. When the area was first harvested, the tree was left standing as there was no safe way to move it. By the late 1930s, new equipment, tools, and practices made the attempt possible. A crane with a lift rating of 12 tons was used to lift the sections onto railroad cars. For safety reasons, the sections were shorter than normal. Community members gathered to have their pictures taken and say good-bye.

One section of the log was cut into two-foot cross sections to be put on display at different places in the Northwest. One section went to the Forest Service Northwest Research Center at Wind River, Washington. Another slice was shared with the Portland exposition building. Another slice was installed at the Pack Demonstration Forest Gate House, where it still can be seen. (Ollie Calvin estate.)

The Storm King Hotel was one of four hotels on Mineral's Front Street. The hotels were the residences of the men working in the three Mineral mills and the mine in Ladd. It was located in the open space between the Headquarters Tavern and American Legion Hall. The people sitting on the porch are not identified. This photograph was taken around 1908. (Jim Hale.)

Jim Hale discusses the advantages of his 1937 British Aston Martin with the unseen photographer. The picture was taken on Sherman Street, and the building still stands. Hale was living in one of the few apartments in town that was not controlled by a mill. There is about a foot of snow on the car. This was photograph was taken just before Hale entered the Navy in 1942. (Jim Hale.)

This is an all-school photograph taken in 1931 or 1932. All of these students fit into the eight classrooms. The population started to decline soon after the picture was taken. The Depression, falling demand for lumber, and new technology in forestry reduced the number of workers needed. (Jim Hale.)

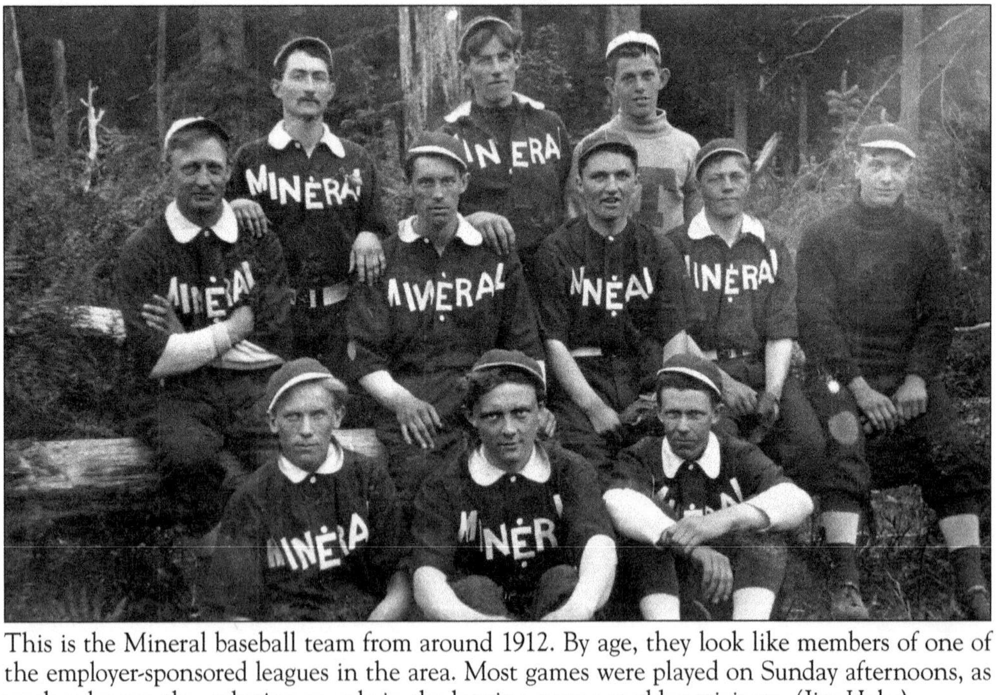

This is the Mineral baseball team from around 1912. By age, they look like members of one of the employer-sponsored leagues in the area. Most games were played on Sunday afternoons, as weekends were the only time people in the logging camps could participate. (Jim Hale.)

The Mineral Hotel, seen here in 1911, was on Front Street across from where the current Mineral Market gas pumps are located. The hotel was favored by the workers of the M.R. Smith Shingle Company. Shingle weavers were considered to be highly skilled workers compared to the general lumber mill workers. Shingle weavers suffered a high rate of industrial injuries to their hands, fingers, and thumbs. (Jim Hale.)

These fishermen have had a successful opening day (now the last Saturday in April) in 1974. The fish are rainbow trout, which may have come from a hatchery. Hatchery expenses come from revenues raised by the sale of fishing licenses. Recent standards are a five fish a day limit. The men are standing on the docks of the Dunlap's Mineral Lake Resort. (Dunlap family.)

Dunlap's Mineral Lake Resort started with the rental of boats in 1948. This is a view of the resort in the early 1950s. There are cabins to rent on the left and docks on the lake where boats were rented, and the store on the right sold snacks for the fish and fishermen. The resort continues to serve the freshwater fishing community. (Dunlap family.)

By the early 1920s, facilities inside the park were straining to house all the visitors. This 12-seat Buick convertible served as a stage transporting guests from Mineral, Elbe, and Ashford to Paradise Valley. The stage left early in the morning and dropped hikers with their sack lunches off at trailheads. In the evening, the stage met the weary hikers for transportation back. (TPL G76_1_067.)

The Mineral Lake Lodge was completed in 1906 by a crew of Scandinavian artisans living in Mineral. The lodge was sold many times and served many purposes over the last century. For a while, it was used as a retreat for the leadership of the Milwaukee Road. At times, it served as a sanatorium for a select clientele and the headquarters for West Fork Logging. It is now a bed-and-breakfast. (Jim Hale.)

William Bevin had his home on the lake. He came to Mineral to lead the miners working the coal works up East Creek at Ladd. When that mine closed, Bevin soon found other work. He was an avid hunter, and he and his dog would go after bear, cougar, quail, and ducks. (Blodwen Truitt.)

This postcard was distributed by the Tacoma Eastern Railroad to encourage tourists to spend a little time on the quiet shores of Mineral Lake. The card was printed in color and was very attractive. Mineral did not develop as much more than a weekend fishing spot until the early

1990s. Then the local Lions Club developed a campground catering to seasonal residents and recreational vehicles. (Linda Lewis.)

Ladd was a small coal mining village to the west of Mineral. The village was about three-quarters of a mile down East Creek from the mine. Debris had clogged the creek and formed a dam. Heavy rains and flooding broke the dam, and the rush of water washed through the village, killing three. (Blodwen Truitt.)

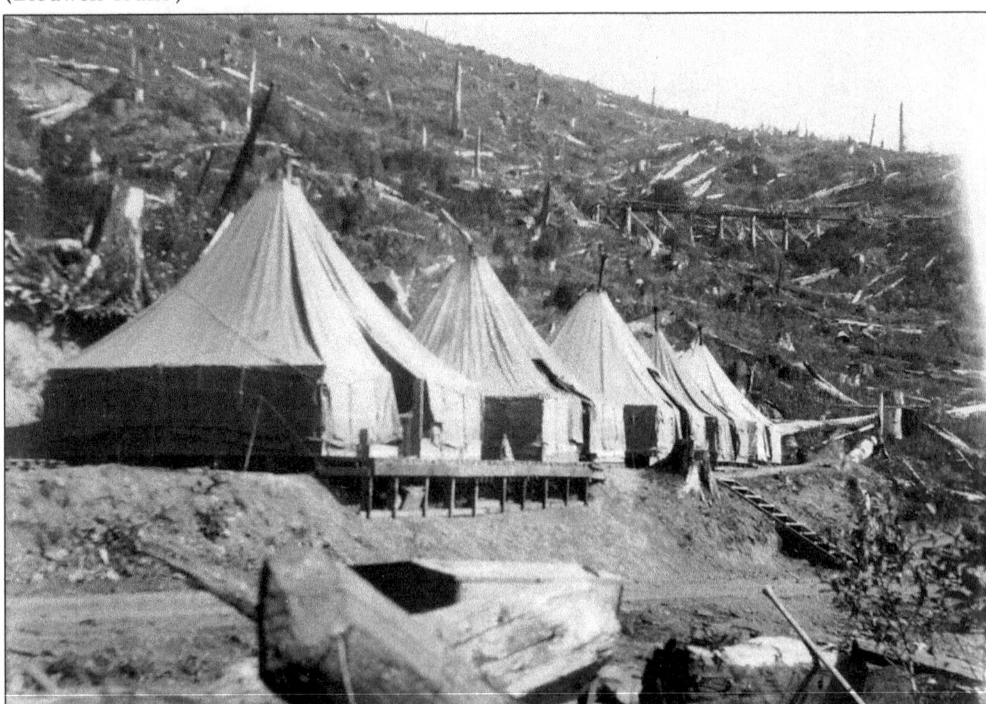

This may be an outpost for the Civilian Conservation Corps (CCC) near Mineral. The hillside behind the tents is what thousands of acres looked like after forest harvesting at the start of the 20th century. A major focus of the CCC was to clear the land of slash and plant millions of seedlings to help the forest to recover. Most of the places now seen by travelers on the byway are replanted forest. (Jim Hale.)

Five

FORESTRY

Before 1900, the woods were thick and nearly impossible to cross. Early roads went around the trees. Making a straight road or a patch for a garden required felling some trees and then removing the stumps. Stumps were set afire, and some roots were cut by ax. Horses or oxen, if available, were used for the final pull and removal. (Marie Fore estate.)

Things changed by 1905. The Tacoma Eastern Railroad entered the valley, seeking timber for market. For the Hale family in Flynn, this meant that their timber had some commercial value. Pictured here is the result of several months of work for the father, J.D. A log for a railroad tie was about nine feet long, nine inches wide, and seven inches high. It had to be flat on two sides and located within eight feet of the proposed track. Payment was $50 per thousand. (Jim Hale.)

In a few years, the process for forest harvesting was systemized with many specialists; the first to arrive was the "cruiser," who estimated the inventory of the area to be harvested. Here, in 1980, a cruiser estimates the number of trees of each species, as each had its own value. The average height and girth were calculated. His report was expressed in board feet. This set the value of the timber. (UofW Pack Forest.)

A forest engineer, seen here in 1949, looks over the area to be harvested. He calculates the cost of harvesting the timber. There are roads to build, camps to construct, water to be found, and crews to be hired. He planned how the work would be sequenced. If the cruiser calculated value, the engineer calculated cost. His report went to the buyer, so a sale price could be negotiated and potential profit could be projected. (TPL RS A443349.)

When an agreement of sale had been reached, work started on the infrastructure. In 1925, a steam shovel is clearing a route for a logging railbed. Hills will be lowered and draws filled or bridged. The grade requirement was that the rise could not be greater than 6 feet over 100 feet of travel (6 percent). (T. Murray.)

By the late 1930s, bulldozers had taken over most of the road, track bed, or trail building. They worked much faster, required fewer crew, and could go up and down steeper grades. Here, a unit originally used for the building of Grand Coulee Dam opens a road to a new landing. (T. Murray.)

Bridges were some of the first construction on a road or railbed. A suitable site for a bridge could influence the placement of the road. Often, a bridge was required so other units could move forward. Most bridges were temporary. When work in an area was completed, the tracks, and then the bridges, were removed and erected somewhere else. This bridge was photographed in 1937. (T. Murray.)

If a camp was required, it might be moved in by rail. This little village had bunkhouses, dining hall, store, recreational facilities, bathhouse, shops, and offices. The building may be erected on skids and lifted on and off flatcars. Sometimes, the cabins were never lifted off the flatcars. Stairs were built to give access. This photograph was taken in November 1922. (TPL B6900.)

In this 1963 photograph, a rigger has topped a Douglas fir that will be used as a spar tree. The rigger can be seen hanging on by his spurs and belt near where he cut the top off the tree. He will be busy over the next several days installing guy wires, pulleys, and other attachments. (TPL WO139511-A.)

Soon, riggers arrive to establish a spar pole, which started as strong trees that had a good view of the land below. It would allow for a log to be lifted off the ground and drawn to a central point. A rigger would clear off branches and then top the tree where the trunk was about 10 inches across. The riggers attached cables for stabilization, like for a radio tower.

Spar poles lift cables off the ground. Controlled by a steam-powered donkey, the cables are on drums or winches and provide "for-and-aft" action. Other cables may control other actions, such as lift and lower. These logs have had the uphill end lifted 10 to 20 feet off the ground and pulled to the pole. The donkey that controls the cables can be seen to the left. (T. Murray.)

Donkeys came in different sizes, with different purposes. This duplex model has seven drums. It could be used to draw logs from a mile or more away and load railroad cars at the same time. This large unit had a crew of seven to service the firewood and water needs of the boiler. This picture was taken in 1937. (T. Murray.)

A mid-sized donkey could be rigged to perform multiple functions; here, it works as a yarder and loader. There are four men pictured near their unit. Two of the men might be needed to cut firewood that is stacked to the left. The operator sits so he can see the cables. The fourth man would be employed releasing the cable from the logs that were moved. (T. Murray.)

Here, a small donkey is used to perform a single function: yarding. It was owned by the Boettcher family who lived near Alder. A small donkey could be rerigged to perform other functions such as loading or moving log cars on the track for loading. With additional plumbing and attachments, the steam donkey could serve as a small mill, such as a tie mill.

The Boettcher Mill near Alder uses a donkey to control a pole that is used to lift logs off a railroad car at the mill. There are eight cables and at least two pulleys on the pole. The reach of the pole is obtained by allowing the top of the pole to drop down or pulling it more upright.

The felling teams may start their work before the spar poles are set. They cut the trees so that the tops are pointed away from the pole. Two men will saw, and one will place wedges in the cut to keep it open and not bind the saw, or use kerosene to remove pitch from the saw teeth. The team will cut the log to length and remove branches.

These fallers are standing on springboards, which were an innovation that resolved several issues. Tree often have a large misshaped trunk near the ground. Fallers need secure footing and space around the tree to work the saw. Using springboards, fallers can start the cut above the butt without squatting or stretching, have their feet flat and solid, and have room to work the saw around trees on hillsides.

Several early Mineral settlers have come together to harvest some timber. This 1904 photograph shows the six horses doing the pulling. The horses are having to step over logs that have been placed so the log they are pulling can "skid" over them, avoiding becoming a plow on the roads—thus the term *skid road* and the phrase "grease the skids." (Jim Hale.)

After the 1960s, more of the yarding work was done with bulldozers. This Caterpillar is equipped with an arch trailer. This lifted the forward end of the log so that it did not plow the track. (T. Murray.)

This is a very early loading dock around 1905. The oxen are moving a log on skids. In the dock area, the oxen step over the dock logs until they are aligned with the empty railcar. The logs are then rolled onto the cars. As the front and back wheels are not attached, they are adjusted for each log's length. (TPL CNC05.)

This is an early logging truck used by Wilson Logging Co. This is an example of the introduction of new technology into forestry. The trucks and roads they needed were less expensive than trains, especially for smaller units. They were a common sight by the 1920s. They usually were underpowered and had an open cab and hard rubber tires, but they could go places that locomotives could not. (TPL B82240.)

From 1890 until the mid-1950, railcars were the main means of transporting logs from the woods to the mills. Better roads, better equipment, and smaller sale units eroded rail's position.

These log cars must be at a reload or mill. They do not have "wrappers," which are chains or cables used to prevent the logs from moving. During World War I, unsecured loads caused several fatal accidents on the intercity routes. (TPL Boland 17067.)

This loader has replaced a steam donkey. It could collect a log from a pile and load it in one action. The boom was designed so that the log could butt against it. The tracks would allow the loader to reposition between steps. The log is being loaded on a St. Regis truck that is not legal for state highways. The trailer is 12 feet wide and could carry loads of up to 100,000 pounds. This photograph was taken in October 1956. (TPL CNC 05.)

Dick Taylor brings the last of the old-growth logs into the yard at Vale. The timber was harvested on the Busy Wild Creek and transported on the Weyerhaeuser Haul Road that allowed the off-road trucks to bypass Eatonville. A section of the haul road remains as Weyerhaeuser Avenue and leads to the Lynch Creek Quarry. The photograph was taken on October 5, 1970.

Ben Cheney, a Tacoma businessman, leased parts of the National Mill site. He set up a small mill to produce eight-foot-long two-by-four studs. It had been noted that when much of the area had first been harvested, logs less than 20 feet in length were considered worthless. Cheney sent crews out to salvage these shorter logs, which proved very profitable. Pictured here is the electrical saw used at National. This headrig was much shorter than most. It also had hydraulic arms to turn the log as needed. (TPL D42837-25.)

After a log has been milled, it is ready for market as lumber. These men are loading some cants from the truck, to a deck, and then onto the railcar. The cants could be recut to produce four studs. These men are using hooks to speed the process. This was in 1949, before the forklift and containers were widely adopted. (TPL D36255-20.)

Stacks of railroad ties are ready for export on the docks in Tacoma. During World War II, much of the lumber production of the Nisqually and Cowlitz Valleys went into the production of ties. There were many small tie mills in the hills. For each mile of rail line, over 5,000 ties are used. These were photographed in November 1951. They were probably destined to rebuild railroads in Asia or Europe. (TPL D62150-8.)

Early in the 20th century, there was little effort to clean up debris after harvesting. Short chunks of logs, treetops, and branches were left where they fell. Scientific research demonstrated that there was use for the shorter logs in other non-lumber processes, such as paper and fiberboard. The litter could inhibit new forest growth. (TPL D229845.)

This is a view of an early commercial cut near National in 1910. Note that many snags were left standing. This was not for some environmental reason as is done today, but because there was no profit in removing them. Forest practice regulation now establishes what needs to happen after harvesting is completed. (Laurie Anderson.)

In 1924, a fire started in a harvesting project near the town of Alder. The fire came close to destroying Eatonville. This is a section of the burn that was added to Pack Forest. It was used as a test bed for learning how to help a forest recover after a fire. (UofW Pack Forest.)

Here, a group of students from the University of Washington School of Forestry plants seedlings in an area burned in a fire. They planted in different patterns and separations to see what growth differences would occur. In this c. 1929 image, the snags are visible in the background. (UofW Pack Forest.)

In August 1888, the famed conservationist and writer John Muir visited Mount Rainier. He followed the trail established by Indian Henry, other Native Americans, and early settlers of the Nisqually Valley. At Longmire Spring, he met up with P.B. Van Trump, one of the first two men to climb the Mountain; A.C. Warner, who took the first photographs from the summit; and several other distinguished men for an ascent, which was achieved on August 11. In writing about other mountains that he loved (and applicable to Mount Rainier), Muir wrote, "The mountains are calling and I must go." (TPL A11606024.)

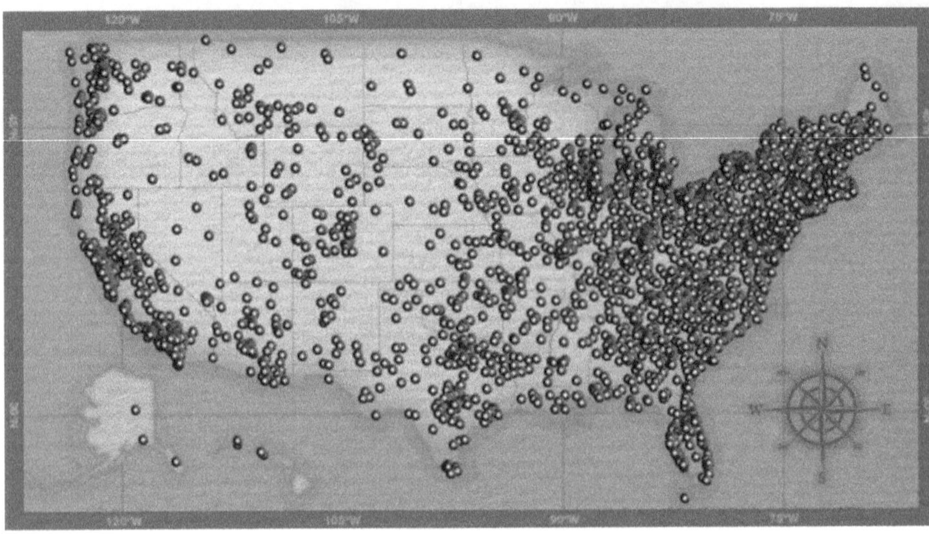

Consistent with our mission to preserve history on a local level, this book was printed in South Carolina on American-made paper and manufactured entirely in the United States. Products carrying the accredited Forest Stewardship Council (FSC) label are printed on 100 percent FSC-certified paper.

MADE IN THE USA

www.ingramcontent.com/pod-product-compliance
Lightning Source LLC
LaVergne TN
LVHW070820030926
847199LV00039B/509

* 9 7 8 1 4 6 7 1 2 9 2 8 2 *